★ GREAT ASTRONOMERS

Jenny Armstrong and Mike Roberts

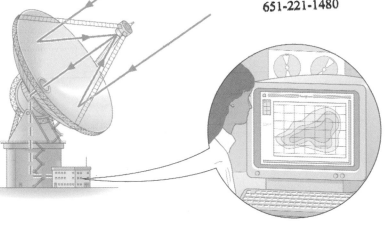

PACIFIC
L E A R N I N G

© 2004 **Pacific Learning**
© 2002 Written by **Jenny Armstrong** and **Mike Roberts**
Photography: AMANDA Project: p. 70; Apache Point Observatory: p. 78;
Astronomical Society of the Pacific: pp. 48, 66, 69; Bridgeman Art Library:
pp. 7, 14, 37; Carnegie Institute, Washington: pp. 58, 59; Corbis UK Ltd.:
p. 33; Corbis UK Ltd./Bettmann: pp. 8, 18, 21, 23, 27, 31, 44; Corbis UK
Ltd./James Sugar: p. 34; Corbis UK Ltd./Paulo Ragazzini: p. 15; Corbis UK
Ltd./Roger Ressmeyer/NASA: p. 75; Corbis UK Ltd./Janet Wishnetsky: p. 6;
Corbis UK Ltd./Adam Woolfit: p. 5; John Frost Newspapers: p. 54; Heritage
Image Partnership: pp. 28, 41; Hulton Getty: pp. 20, 42, 43, 46; MACHO
Project: p. 70; NASA: pp. 74, 77; Photodisc: p. 4; Popperfoto: p. 51;
Retrograph: pp. 55, 56; Ann Ronan Picture Library: p. 64; Scala: p. 35;
Science Photo Library/Jean-Loup Charmet: pp. 24, 38; Science Photo
Library/NASA: p. 73; Martin Sookias: p. 61.
Front cover: Heritage Image Partners; back cover: Apache Point Observatory
Illustrations are by: Stefan Chabluk, Richard Morris, and Thomas Sperling.
The authors would like to thank Reverend Tymothy Edge for his advice on
this project.
U.S. edit by **Rebecca McEwen**

This Americanized Edition of *Great Astronomers,* originally published in
England in 2002, is published by arrangement with Oxford University Press

13 12 11 10
10 9 8 7 6 5 4 3 2

Published by
Pacific Learning
P.O. Box 2723
Huntington Beach, CA 92647-0723
www.pacificlearning.com

ISBN: 978-1-59055-452-4
PL-7616

Printed in China through Colorcraft Ltd., Hong Kong

Contents

Introduction

When we look up into the night sky, we see, more or less, the same things as people who lived 10,000 years ago, or even one million years ago. Even though our picture is very similar to theirs, our understanding of it is completely different.

In the ancient world, people believed that the Earth was the center of the universe. They used the stars to monitor the seasons, to help them navigate the seas, and to predict what was going to happen on Earth. The ancient Egyptians noticed that the stars moved in a regular pattern every 365 days,

A pair of ordinary modern binoculars is more powerful than Galileo's strongest telescope.

so they divided up their calendar year into 365 days.

Today, we know that Earth is just one planet in one solar system in one galaxy in the whole universe. We have also learned that the universe is enormous and expanding; the vast distances between stars can be measured in light-years, and what we see is just a tiny fraction of what is actually out there.

The remains of Stonehenge in England. Many people believe the **prehistoric** stone circles were set up to track movements of the Sun and Moon, and also the seasons.

This stone beehive-style building in Korea may be the earliest surviving observatory. It has a central opening in the roof for looking at the stars.

Today, the more scientists study and learn about the universe, the more we realize how little we know about it.

This book looks at some of the great **astronomers** who have helped us expand our knowledge of the universe. Their theories were not always correct – although many of them made amazing advances that allowed more modern astronomers to figure out the truth.

Sometimes the astronomers who lived long ago formulated ideas that made them unpopular, or even put them in great danger.

Yet without the courage and insight of these pioneers, we would not have the knowledge that we have today.

*An **astrolabe***

An astrolabe in use

Chapter 1
Aristotle (384–322 BC)

The ideas and writings of the ancient Greek philosopher, Aristotle, helped to shape the very way people thought about the universe for nearly 2,000 years.

Learning and Teaching

As a young man, Aristotle was sent to study at the academy in Athens, where he was taught by the brilliant philosopher Plato. He continued his studies abroad and then took up teaching. One of his pupils was Alexander, son of the ruler of Greece. Alexander went on to become a powerful leader, later known as Alexander the Great.

Earth at the Center of the Universe

Aristotle, like many ancient Greek philosophers, tried to explain the universe through logic and reason, rather than through myths and legends. In Aristotle's now famous books, *On the Heavens* and *Physics*, he explained some of his beliefs about the universe.

He believed that the Earth could be considered the true center of the

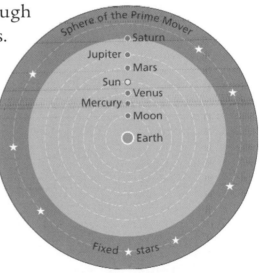

Aristotle's geocentric (Earth-at-the-center) view of the universe

universe, surrounded by the starry heavens in the shape of a sphere. Whereas the Earth was full of change and turmoil, Aristotle believed that the heavens – which he called the firmament – were permanently fixed and unchanging. Between the Earth and the heavens, Aristotle described the Sun, Moon, and planets as beings that rotated around the all-important Earth.

Wandering Planets

"Planets" means "wanderers" in ancient Greek. They were named "planets" because early astronomers saw that they moved in irregular patterns – they appeared to "wander" in the night sky. Although puzzled by these movements, few people doubted that the Earth was fixed at the center of the universe.

Aristotle's views about the position of the Earth and the heavens were accepted for 2,000 years, until scientists gained more understanding about the laws of motion and

gravity. It was not until better astronomical instruments were developed that people could see there was a parallax effect. It was just too small to see with the naked eye

The Parallax Effect

The parallax effect is when an object appears to move if you view it from different positions. For example, try viewing a finger with one eye shut and then the other eye shut: the finger appears to move. The farther from your eye, the smaller the apparent movement.

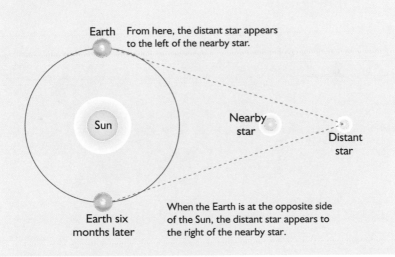

Earth — From here, the distant star appears to the left of the nearby star.

Sun

Nearby star

Distant star

Earth six months later — When the Earth is at the opposite side of the Sun, the distant star appears to the right of the nearby star.

Even though Aristotle gained great fame for his ideas, there were still a few people who disagreed with him.

Aristarchos was one of the very few astronomers who questioned Aristotle's geocentric view of the universe. In about 298 BC, Aristarchos devised a new theory that he called the heliocentric, or Sun-at-the-center, view of the universe. He made the bold suggestion that the Earth orbited the sun, and spun on its own axis.

As strange as it may now seem, many people laughed at Aristarchos. They argued

that if the Earth spun on its axis, why didn't objects fly off the Earth and into the firmament?

Then, they demanded to know how – if the Earth really was moving – it didn't leave behind birds that were flying in the air.

Last but not least, they wonderd how the Earth could possibly be moving around the Sun, since the stars in the night sky still seemed to be in the same relative positions. In other words, why wasn't there a parallax effect for the stars?

Chapter 2

Claudius Ptolemy (AD 100–170)

Known as the "Prince of Astronomers," Ptolemy was the greatest astronomer of his time.

Life and Work

Ptolemy lived in the Egyptian city of Alexandria. He was a talented scientist, whose life's work covered geography, **optics**, and **astrology**, in addition to astronomy.

When the Roman Empire collapsed in the fourth century, much learning was lost as libraries and books were burned by invaders. Fortunately, Ptolemy's work had been translated into Arabic. While Europe was plunged into the **Dark Ages**, the science of astronomy was kept alive in the great civilizations of Islam.

Ptolemy's model of the universe showed a series of circles, representing the orbits of the planets around the Earth.

The *Almagest*

Ptolemy's most important work was a collection of thirteen books known as the *Almagest*. In this work, Ptolemy wrote: "We shall try to note down everything which we think we have discovered up to the present time... to avoid undue length we shall merely recount what has been adequately established by the Ancients. However, those topics which have not been dealt with by our predecessors at all will be discussed at length to the best of our ability."

This extract from a sixteenth-century translation of the "Almagest" lists the stars in the Orion **constellation**, gives their positions, and rates them according to their brightness.

The *Almagest* explained Aristotle's ideas of a geocentric universe, predicted the positions of the planets for many years to come, and also contained a catalog of 1,028 stars.

Imperfect Orbits

Although the planets' orbits were usually drawn as perfect circles, astronomers had been puzzled for centuries by observations that showed these orbits were irregular. Sometimes the planets appeared to move backward, then forward again. Also, their brightness varied. Ptolemy explained the "imperfect" orbits with a theory that the planets moved in **epicycles** (small circles) within their orbits.

Ptolemy said the Earth was still the center of the universe... just not the exact center!

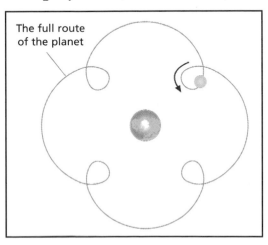

The full route of the planet

Chapter 3

Nicolaus Copernicus

(1473–1543)

Nicolaus Copernicus brought astronomy out of the Dark Ages. He suggested that the Sun, not the Earth, was the center of the universe. Although Copernicus's innovative work was not recognized in his own lifetime, it led the way for important discoveries in the future.

Early Life

Copernicus was born in Poland, and from childhood he took his studies very seriously. He was interested in mathematics, Greek, medicine, and religious law.

He became a Catholic priest, but he spent much of his spare time studying the stars and reading works written by the ancient Greek astronomers.

The Copernican Revolution

Copernicus's ideas were based more on his reading than his observations. What puzzled him most about Ptolemy's idea of the universe was why the planets' movements were so irregular. He took up Aristarchos's theories about the Sun-centered universe (see pages 12–13). If the Earth and other planets orbited the Sun, this would explain some of the "wanderings" in the planets' movements. Copernicus pointed out that, if it took the Earth twenty-four hours to rotate (turn on its axis), this would explain night and day.

In some ways, Copernicus was an unusual "revolutionary." Although his ideas about the solar system, with the Sun at the center, were startling, he was very cautious about discussing these. In fact, he talked about them with only a few people, and always in a private setting. He wrote a book about his ideas called *De Revolutionibus*. Written in Latin, which was the language of learning at the time, it was filled with his observations

A page from an early manuscript version of "De Revolutionibus," before it was published.

and theories. Copernicus did not publish his book until he was dying, in 1543. However, before that time, his assistant persuaded him to write down his ideas, which were then given to people anonymously.

Sun   Earth   Zodiac

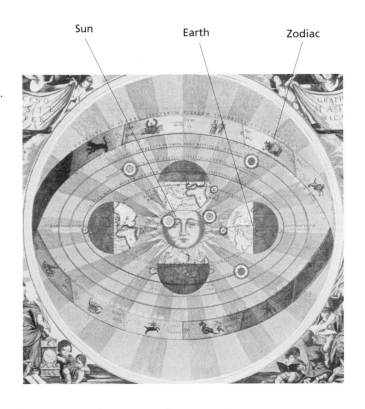

Copernicus's view of the solar system. This seventeenth-century print shows Copernicus's theory about the six known planets orbiting around the Sun.

The Christian Church

The Church had accepted Ptolemy's idea that the Earth was the center of the universe, because it fit in with the Church's teachings about the creation of the Earth and the heavens. Copernicus knew that his new ideas might anger the Church, which was why he was reluctant to publish his work. Like most medieval scientists and scholars, Copernicus depended on the support of the Church for books, work, and money.

Copernicus struggled with the conflict between his religion and his scientific beliefs for the rest of his life. He became a canon, which was an important position in the Church, but refused to become a bishop. He felt it would leave him too little time to study astronomy.

Chapter 4

Tycho Brahe (1546–1601)

Tycho Brahe observed and catalogued more than 1,000 stars. He did this by building sensitive scientific instruments that let him see more than ten times the detail of any previous observations.

Early Life

Tycho Brahe was the oldest son of a wealthy Danish family who sent him to a university, at the young age of thirteen, to study law. However, when he saw an **eclipse** of the Sun in 1560, he became fascinated with the science of astronomy, particularly with predictions about the movements of the planets. Despite his family's disapproval, he spent most of his time and money on astronomy.

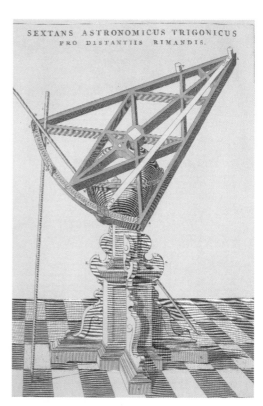

*Before telescopes, astronomers used measuring instruments, such as this **sextant**, to map the stars.*

Brahe's headstrong attitude about his course of study wasn't too surprising. He was known for being impulsive and competitive. An argument with another student about who was the better mathematician led to a duel in which Brahe lost part of his nose. After this, he wore an artificial nose made out of gold and silver.

A New Star

In 1572, Brahe noticed a brilliant new star, which was so bright that it could be seen in daylight. The nova (new star) caused great surprise because ever since the time of Aristotle, people had believed that stars were fixed and unchanging in the heavens. Brahe used his large, newly built sextant to measure the position of the new star. He proved that it was far beyond the Earth's atmosphere.

The Castle of the Heavens

Brahe gave lectures and published his work. By 1575, he was famous throughout

Europe. Proud of his achievements, the King of Denmark gave Brahe the island of Hven and money to build an observatory. Brahe then built his "Castle of the Heavens," which contained several observatories, a laboratory, and a library.

In the library, Brahe installed a brass globe, five feet (1.5 m) in diameter. During the next twenty years, as he measured and observed the stars, he engraved them onto the globe.

In Brahe's study, a huge quadrant was set up next to a window, through which he could make his observations. With a team of assistants, many sets of instruments, and clocks, Brahe recorded more accurate measurements of the stars than had ever been made before.

By 1597, Brahe had argued with the new Danish king, so he left Hven and went to live and study in Prague, in Bohemia.

Although many of Brahe's ideas were wrong (for example, he believed that the Sun moved around the Earth), he was correct in thinking that the other planets moved around the Sun. His careful measurements and records of the stars and planets were important to future astronomers.

A painting of Tycho Brahe in his observatory

Johannes Kepler (1571–1630)

Johannes Kepler had a brilliant mind. By looking carefully at some of Tycho Brahe's data, he made some startling discoveries.

Early Life

Johannes Kepler was born in southwest Germany. While he was studying at a university, he proved himself brilliant in mathematics and astronomy. His tutor, Michael Maestlin, taught him astronomy according to Ptolemy's theories (with the Earth at the center of the universe), but Kepler privately believed in Copernicus's theories (with the Sun at the center). Kepler began to support Copernicus's ideas, but this made him unpopular with the university authorities.

Drawing an Ellipse

Push two pins into a board and link them with a loop of thread. Place a pencil inside the loop and stretch it, moving it around both pins. This makes an ellipse. Each pin is called a focus. In each planet's elliptical orbit in the solar system, the Sun is at one focus.

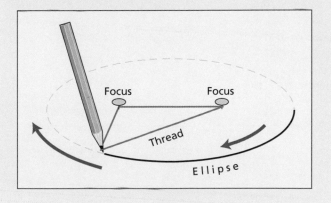

Kepler didn't care if his ideas made him unpopular. He believed that his own work confirmed Copernicus's theories about the Sun being at the center of the universe. He urged fellow astronomers, such as Galileo, to publish their work to support these ideas.

Discovering How Planets Move

In 1600, Kepler was invited to work as Tycho Brahe's assistant in Prague. Brahe was the best-known astronomer of his time, and

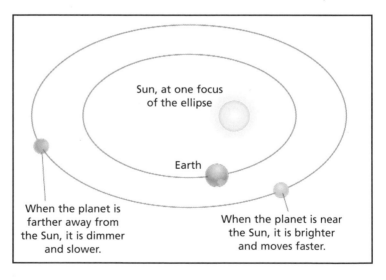

Sun, at one focus of the ellipse

Earth

When the planet is farther away from the Sun, it is dimmer and slower.

When the planet is near the Sun, it is brighter and moves faster.

Kepler discovered that the speed of each planet varies during its orbit.

Kepler was eager to see the huge amount of information he had collected. However, Brahe kept most of his records to himself and suggested that Kepler just look at the information he had collected about Mars. This, in fact, was all Kepler needed to make the calculations that led to an important new discovery – that the orbit of Mars was elliptical (oval-shaped) and not circular.

Kepler explaining his discovery of planetary motion to his sponsor, Emperor Rudolph II

This discovery was important because it explained the wandering movements of the planets that had puzzled astronomers since ancient times. In ancient Greece, Ptolemy had explained them with his theory of epicycles, but Kepler, using Brahe's data, proved this was wrong.

Kepler's Laws

Brahe died in 1601, and Kepler took possession of all his books and records immediately. Using Brahe's data, Kepler figured out three mathematical laws that explained the movements of the planets around the Sun. He showed that their orbits were elliptical and that their speed changed during orbit. He also linked the distances of the planets from the Sun with the time they took to make a single orbit.

Galileo Galilei (1564–1642)

Galileo was the first astronomer to use a telescope to study the stars. What he saw changed people's view of the universe forever.

Galileo's Telescopes

Galileo was a mathematics professor at Padua University in Italy when he heard that a new scientific instrument had been invented. The instrument was a tube with two lenses that made things look bigger.

Galileo was fascinated by this idea and soon had made his own telescope. He turned it toward the sky and found that he could see the planets and stars more clearly than ever before.

Galileo's first telescope made objects look three times larger than normal. Later, he made more powerful telescopes: one of them made objects look thirty times larger.

One of Galileo's telescopes

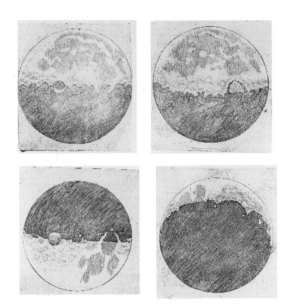

Galileo drew these sketches of the Moon, after making a series of observations through his telescope. They were published in his book "Messenger of the Stars" in 1610.

New Discoveries

With his telescope, Galileo made some startling discoveries. He saw four moons circling the planet Jupiter; the "ears" of Saturn (which we now know are rings of dust and ice particles); sunspots on the Sun; and mountains and craters on the Moon. He also observed the planet Venus changing shape gradually, like the Moon, from a full sphere to a crescent, and back again.

Galileo realized that all these things proved that the Church was wrong in teaching that the Earth was the center of the universe, with all the planets circling around it in perfect spheres. Clearly, Jupiter was being circled by its own moons, Venus appeared to change shape because it was circling around the Sun, and the variations on the surfaces of the Sun and Moon meant they were not in fact perfect "heavenly bodies."

The Church Fights Back

Although a few other scientists, such as Copernicus, had suggested that the Earth was not the center of the universe, the Church had not been alarmed because the whole idea had seemed so unlikely.

Galileo, however, was seen as a dangerous threat because he was a highly respected scientist and people believed him. He published his work in Italian, so that ordinary people could read about his

This painting shows Galileo in the Church Court in 1616. Although the court convicted and imprisoned him, it could not keep news of his discoveries from spreading.

discoveries, rather than in Latin, which was the language used by the Church and universities.

In 1616, the Church forced Galileo to appear in court. They threatened to torture him unless he said that his ideas were wrong. Galileo had no choice but to agree. His books were banned, and he was imprisoned in his house for the rest of his life.

Chapter 7

Isaac Newton (1642–1727)

More than any other scientist, Isaac Newton increased our understanding of how things move on Earth and in space. He has been described as "the father of modern science."

Laws of Motion

While Isaac Newton was professor of mathematics at Cambridge University in England, he made detailed studies and calculations about how things moved. He came to the conclusion that objects moved according to three main ideas (these became known as Newton's "laws of motion"). At the center of these laws was the idea that any

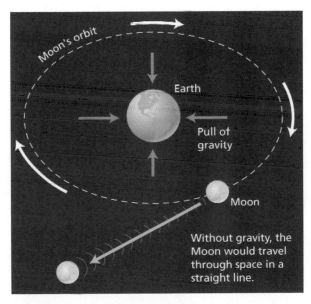

Gravity keeps the Moon in orbit around the Earth.

object will keep moving in a straight line unless it is interrupted by a force, and that when an object is still, it has stopped moving because of a force. For example, a ball stops rolling because of air resistance and friction.

Gravity

Studying how and why things moved led Newton to a theory of gravity. Many people have heard the story that says Newton came up with the idea of gravity after an apple fell out of a tree and hit him on the head.

Although nobody knows for sure whether this is the exact truth, watching an apple fall may have given Newton the idea that there could be a force like gravity.

Newton eventually proved, through many observations and calculations, that all objects are pulled together by the force of gravity. Smaller objects are pulled toward larger objects (for example, an apple is pulled toward the Earth). Massive objects in motion, such as planets and moons, can be pulled by gravity into orbit around even larger objects. Without gravity, the Moon would travel through space in a straight line.

Newton's Telescope

In addition to studying the movement of objects, Newton was also interested in light and optics. He developed a new type of telescope, using mirrors made from polished metal instead of lenses.

This design made the telescope a much more powerful tool. Newton's telescope was shorter than previous designs and gave a clearer image. Details of the invention were published in 1671, and Newton became famous throughout Europe.

Helpful Assistance

Newton was encouraged in his work by a fellow British astronomer, Edmund Halley (1656–1742), who was particularly interested in comets. He studied records of their appearance and traced their orbits, using Newton's ideas about gravity.

One comet in particular fascinated him. This comet was seen in 1066 during the

Halley's Comet was last seen in 1986.

In 1066, William the Conqueror thought the comet was a sign that Harold would lose the Battle of Hastings.

Battle of Hastings and recorded on a famous piece of art called the Bayeux Tapestry.

Halley proposed that some of the comets were, in fact, the same comet reappearing at regular intervals. His theory was proved when he predicted, correctly, that the 1066 comet would reappear in 1759. It was named Halley's Comet in his honor.

Chapter 8

William and Caroline Herschel (1738–1822 and 1750–1848)

Caroline and William were talented musicians from Hanover in Germany, but they gave up their music to devote more time to astronomy.

A Brother and Sister Team

Unlike other astronomers of their day, William Herschel and his sister Caroline were not content with observing just the nearby planets, the Sun, and the Moon. They wanted to look farther into space, but to do this they needed more powerful telescopes – so they made their own.

In their observatory near Bath, England, they frequently worked through the night. One would observe the stars through the telescope, while the other took detailed notes.

A New Planet

In order to build a telescope that would be powerful enough for their needs, the Herschels ground and polished their own mirrors to use in their telescopes. They realized that the larger the mirror, the more light the telescope would be able to collect, and the more detail they would be able to observe.

In 1781, using his own telescope, William identified a new planet, which he named

Uranus. It was the first planet to be discovered since prehistoric times, and William became famous.

In 1845, Lord Rosse built a seventy-two inch (183 cm) telescope at Birr Castle in Ireland. He used it to observe spiral-shaped nebulae (which are now known to be specific galaxies).

Luminous Nebulae

Through their powerful telescopes, the Herschels studied what appeared to be luminous clouds (nebulae) in the sky. Whereas some astronomers believed that these clouds were a glowing milky fluid or gas, the Herschels identified individual stars within them. They suggested that while some of the nebulae were indeed clouds of gas or dust, others might actually be very distant star systems (which are now known as galaxies).

Chapter 9

Henrietta Leavitt (1868–1921)

Henrietta Leavitt discovered how to measure the distance to stars a long way from Earth. Her method of measurement was important for figuring out the real size of the universe, and it is still in use today.

"Winking" Stars

One of the first professional women astronomers, Henrietta Leavitt spent most of her working life at the Harvard College Observatory in Boston, Massachusetts. Much of Leavitt's work was on variable stars. These stars are sometimes bright, sometimes dim, and appear to be slowly "winking" over time.

Leavitt identified more than 2,400 variable stars, about half the known stars in her day.

Cepheid Variables

However, Leavitt's most innovative and important contribution to astronomy was her pioneering work on cepheid variables. These are stars whose brightness changes in a regular pattern.

She figured out how to calculate the distance of these stars by using the speed at which they appear to flash on and off, and then allowing for the fact that more distant stars are less bright than close ones.

Her work went on to influence many other astronomers of the twentieth century.

The Great Debate

In the 1920s, an official debate took place at the Smithsonian Institution in Washington, D.C. Some astronomers (led by a man named Harlow Shapley) argued that the universe was one big galaxy, while others (led by Heber Curtis) argued that the universe was made up of many galaxies similar to our own.

There was disagreement until Edwin Hubble used Leavitt's methods of calculation to study distant nebulae. He confirmed that these were distant galaxies, not just clouds of dust and gas.

Chapter 10

Albert Einstein (1879–1955)

Albert Einstein was one of the greatest scientists of all time. He challenged Newton's laws of physics, suggesting that time, space, and gravity were all interlinked (related). These relativity theories changed the way people thought about the universe.

Early Life

Einstein was born in Germany but followed his family to Italy in 1895, and then completed his education in Switzerland.

He was a brilliant, but unusual, student. Although he was extremely intelligent, Einstein often had arguments with his teachers and was quite unpopular with many academics.

In 1902, he started to work in the Swiss Patent Office, studying projects by some of the country's most talented inventors. In his spare time, Einstein worked on his own scientific ideas.

Relativity

In 1905, Einstein published a paper (which later came to be known as the special theory of relativity) outlining revolutionary new ideas about time and space.

He argued that the speed of light is the same whether the source of light is moving or not, but that time varies according to the

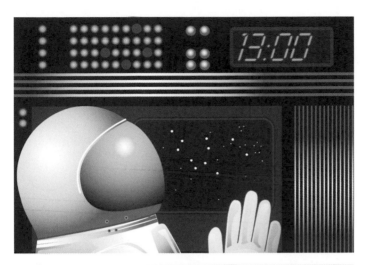

According to Einstein's theory of relativity, astronauts on a voyage traveling close to the speed of light will find that time passes more slowly for them than for people on Earth.

speed of the person measuring time. The faster someone travels, the less time will seem to pass.

Ten years later, Einstein completed his work on relativity with another paper (now known as the general theory of relativity). This proposed that the effects of gravity are due to the curvature of space around objects, kind of like how a trampoline curves when there is a weight on it.

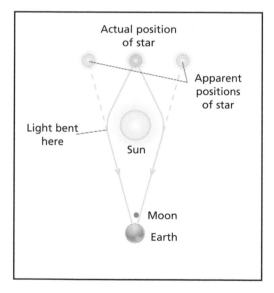

How the Sun's gravity bends a star's light

Einstein's theory of relativity was proven to be correct during the eclipse of the Sun in 1919. Other scientists were able to observe how the light from a star was bent by the Sun's gravity.

Fame

In 1921, Einstein was awarded the Nobel Prize for physics. He became famous not only for his scientific achievements, but also for his stance against the Nazis and his promotion of the ideas of peace, freedom, and justice.

His scientific ideas and political beliefs made him a popular public figure. His photograph was often in newspapers and magazines, and even today he is still one of the most instantly recognized scientists in history.

Einstein believed that scientists have a great responsibility to other people. He said: "Never regard your study as a duty, but as the enviable opportunity to learn [for your own pleasure] and to profit the community to which your work belongs."

$$E = mc$$

This famous equation was figured out for the first time by Einstein.

Einstein knew that before people could work on atomic fission (splitting an atom) and on atomic fusion (joining atoms together), they needed to understand the relationship between energy (E), matter (m), and the speed of light (c).

Today, atomic fission and fusion are used to make nuclear weapons and in the manufacture of nuclear power.

In addition, atomic fission and fusion are what give the Sun its light and heat.

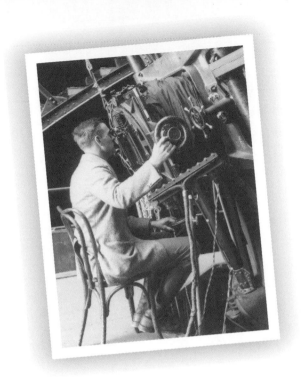

Chapter 11

Edwin Hubble (1884–1953)

Edwin Hubble proved that the universe was far bigger than anyone had previously thought.

Early Life

Born in Missouri, Edwin Hubble originally trained as a lawyer, but his interest in astronomy drew him to work at the largest observatory in the world. This was located at the top of Mount Wilson, near Los Angeles, California.

Measuring Distance in Light-Years

Using the giant Hooker telescope, Hubble studied other galaxies and nebulae (clouds of dust and gas). In 1923, he examined the Andromeda galaxy and discovered "winking" stars similar to those

The Hooker telescope at Mount Wilson, which was famous for its 100-inch (250-cm) mirror

studied by Henrietta Leavitt. Using Leavitt's methods of calculation, Hubble figured out that the Andromeda galaxy was so far away that it was impossible to calculate the distance in miles. Instead, he measured it in light-years. A light-year is the distance that light travels in one year – about 5.9 trillion miles (9.5 trillion km). Hubble figured out that the Andromeda galaxy was more than one million light-years away.

The Expanding Universe

As Hubble began to map the universe, galaxy by galaxy, he also measured how quickly the galaxies were moving. Those farthest away seemed to be moving most quickly. This became known as Hubble's law. Hubble concluded that the universe was expanding.

The Big Bang Theory

Many scientists refused to believe that the universe was expanding. However, in 1927, a Catholic priest, Georges Lemaître, proposed

The theory of the expanding universe can be shown with a balloon. Paint some stars on a balloon, then watch them move farther apart as the balloon is inflated.

that the universe began about fifteen billion years ago, with a huge explosion. This explosion marked the beginning of space, matter, and time, and led to the creation of galaxies, stars, and planets. The Roman Catholic Church supported this theory, as it fit in with its belief of a single moment of creation.

A Meeting of Great Minds

Lemaître believed that the idea of the Big Bang brought together Einstein's theories of relativity with Hubble's theory of the expanding universe. The three men met, and Lemaître explained his ideas in detail.

Following their historic meeting, Einstein remarked that the Big Bang theory was "the most beautiful and satisfying interpretation I have ever listened to."

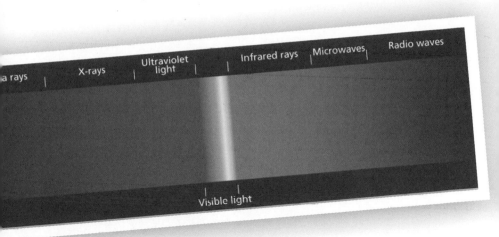

Chapter 12

Radio Astronomers

The light we can see with our eyes is called visible light. It can be split into different colors, which are easiest to see in a rainbow. However, there are other "colors" that humans cannot see, in the same way that there are sounds that humans cannot hear (for example, a dog whistle).

Early astronomers could only observe the universe using visible light. However, the development of radio telescopes in the middle of the twentieth century meant that astronomers could look beyond visible light and begin to learn more about the universe.

Jansky building his antenna receiver

Karl Jansky (1905–1950)

Karl Jansky was an American engineer who worked for Bell Telephone Laboratories. His job was to find out what was causing interference in telephone communications. Jansky built a huge antenna receiver (the first basic radio telescope) and analyzed all the signals he detected. In 1931, he discovered that some of the radio interference he was hearing actually was coming from stars.

Grote Reber (1911–2002)

Another American engineer, Grote Reber, developed Jansky's work and built the first dish-shaped radio receiver. This could detect radio noise coming from galaxies so far away that they were invisible to the naked eye. Jansky began to map out more distant galaxies.

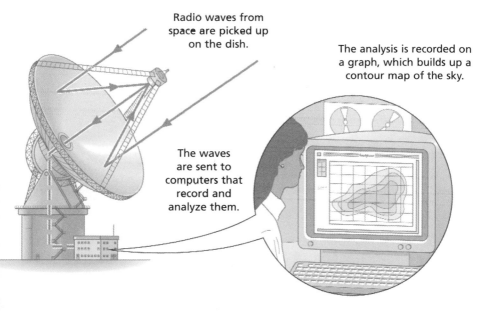

Radio waves from space are picked up on the dish.

The analysis is recorded on a graph, which builds up a contour map of the sky.

The waves are sent to computers that record and analyze them.

How a radio telescope maps the skies

Arno Penzias (born 1933) and Robert Wilson (born 1936)

In 1965, American scientists Penzias and Wilson were doing experiments with a very sensitive radio receiver, but they kept detecting a hissing interference. They realized that the hiss was due to a low level of **radiation**.

Astronomers had been predicting that this radiation would have been left throughout the universe following the Big Bang. This was the best evidence, to date, that the Big Bang had occurred.

Jocelyn Bell at work

Jocelyn Bell (born 1943)

Jocelyn Bell was a young Irish student who was working with her tutor, Anthony Hewish, at Cambridge University in England. Suddenly she noticed regular radio signals from space.

Some people wondered whether these could be signals from other life-forms, but Bell discovered they were coming from rapidly spinning new stars – now known as pulsars. Pulsars throw out radio signals as they spin (in the same way that a lighthouse gives out a beam of light at regular intervals).

Chapter 13

Dark Matter Astronomers

Vera Rubin (born 1928)

Until the twentieth century, astronomers thought that they could eventually see everything in the universe with modern instruments. However, in the 1970s, an American astronomer named Vera Rubin suggested that we see only 10 percent of what actually exists. The other 90 percent is an invisible quantity called dark matter.

Rubin's measurement of the speed of rotating galaxies led her to believe in dark matter – a halo of invisible material

Vera Rubin

surrounding galaxies. Although at first many scientists doubted Rubin's theory, today it is widely accepted. Several teams of astronomers are trying to find out more about dark matter.

MACHO

The MACHO (Massive Compact Halo Object) team is looking for huge stellar bodies with great mass and weight, also

The MACHO team

known as massive black holes. The project involves astronomers working with American and Australian telescopes.

WIMPS

Another team of scientists believes that the dark matter may be WIMPS (Weakly Interacting Massive Particles) – tiny particles that are even smaller than atoms. These particles can be studied not just by looking at the sky, but also by reading the recordings of sensitive equipment that is buried deep in the Antarctic ice.

This equipment can detect any of these tiny particles (neutrinos) that have come from outer space.

In the AMANDA (Antarctic Muon and Neutrino Detector Array) project, detectors are lowered more than half a mile (1 km) below the surface of the Antarctic ice.

Chapter 14

George Smoot (born 1945)

One of the greatest challenges for modern astronomers has been to get clearer pictures of space by setting up telescopes outside the Earth's atmosphere. The atmosphere can distort light and radiation, so telescopes are less effective on Earth.

Adventures in Astronomy

An American **astrophysicist** named George Smoot led a team of scientists who wanted to study the cosmic radiation that was originally left by the Big Bang. At first the team tried mounting telescopes on rockets and balloons, but they suffered numerous

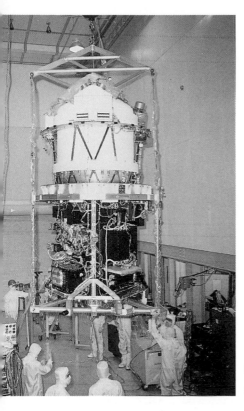

COBE was a radio telescope attached to a satellite.

setbacks. Along the way, they had to search for a lost hot-air balloon in the Badlands of South Dakota, work from a freezing station at the South Pole in Antarctica, and conduct atmosphere tests from a U2 spy plane above the mountains of Peru.

Eventually, they found their greatest success with the Cosmic Background Explorer (COBE) satellite in 1989.

This computer image from COBE shows variations in the radiation from the Big Bang.

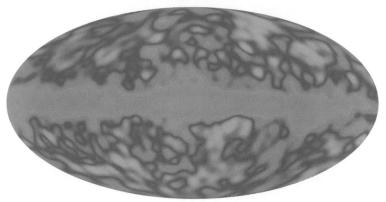

Wrinkles in Time

By 1992, COBE had detected an irregular pattern in the background radiation in the universe (this radiation was first identified by Penzias and Wilson, back in 1965). This "ripple effect" or "wrinkle" was the oldest thing that people had ever discovered within the universe. It was further evidence that the Big Bang had taken place. Scientists agreed that the irregular strings and clumps of radiation had led to the formation of galaxies, stars, and planets.

The *Hubble Space Telescope*

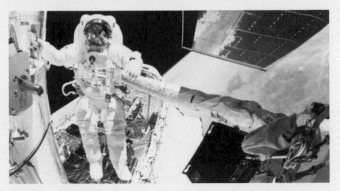

Astronauts repairing the *Hubble* telescope in 1993

The *Hubble Space Telescope* was launched into Earth's orbit in 1990 to take pictures of the universe outside Earth's distorting atmosphere. It is so powerful that if it were above Washington, D.C., it could see a firefly in Tokyo, Japan! It was named as a tribute to Edwin Hubble's work.

In addition to finding the "seeds" that create stars and planets, Smoot and his team found a great deal of interesting information about our galaxy.

According to his data, our planet – and everything around it – is being dragged to a great and unseen **supercluster**... all at a speed of 373 miles (600 km) a second!

Chapter 15

The Future

Great astronomers have expanded our view and understanding of the universe. We can now look deeper and deeper into space, although we know that whatever we see is probably just a fraction of what is out there.

As technology has advanced, we are able to build powerful, sensitive, and much more specialized scientific equipment, but this is very expensive. Individual countries are often unable to afford the expense. As a result, more and more astronomical projects are conducted by two or more countries. For example, the United States and Japan have set

*Part of the Hubble Deep Field image,
which shows more than 3,000 galaxies,
all at different stages of evolution.*

up the Sloan Digital Sky Survey, in order to map more than 100 million stars, one million galaxies, and 100,000 **quasars**.

It may be that the most important astronomers in the future will be robots – the **probes** that are sent out to distant planets and stars. So far, probes such as *Venera*, *Viking*, *Voyager*, and *Galileo* have explored the giant planets in our solar system. Maybe one day, others will travel even farther.

Alternatively, the future may lie with space telescopes, such as the *Hubble Space Telescope*. In 1995, the *Hubble Telescope* spent ten days collecting images from one tiny patch of the sky. The images were put together by computer and the final picture is like a snapshot of the entire history of the universe.

Teams of astronomers around the world are now studying all the information contained in this one amazing picture, the Hubble Deep Field.

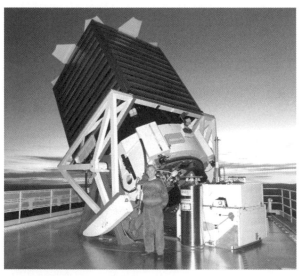

This telescope in New Mexico can see 1.5 billion light-years from Earth!

Glossary

astrolabe – an ancient instrument used for measuring the positions of the stars, Moon, and Sun

astrology – study attempting to link the movement of the stars and planets to what happens on Earth

astronomer – someone who studies the stars, planets, Sun, and Moon

astrophysicist – a scientist who studies a special kind of astronomy, focusing on the behavior and physical makeup of things that exist out in space

constellation – a pattern of stars in the sky

Dark Ages – a time in European history (AD 476–800) after Roman civilization broke down, when much learning and culture was lost

eclipse – what occurs when something moves, and hides an object behind it

epicycle – a small circle around the circumference of a larger circle

gravity – a force that pulls objects together

optics – the science of light

prehistoric – describes times that occurred before people had a written history

probe – a spacecraft that travels far into space to explore, without human crew

quasar – a luminous object in space that may be the center of a distant galaxy

radiation – heat and energy that something produces

sextant – an instrument for measuring angles between stars

supercluster – a massive grouping of galaxies that have come together

Index